DISC
BASIC

Introduction

In the following book you will read about DISC models, assessment tools that provide information on people's personal characteristics and are used to maximize employee performance. It is purposefully written in the plural since there are several DISC models on the market. You may have heard of Extended DISC, Thomas International, Discover Insights, DISK, and so on.

In my professional life, I have worked with the Extended DISC model for more than seven years and have conducted nearly all certification training in Denmark during this period. Besides my role as trainer, I have been advising managers and HR departments and their consultants and partners on how they could use this model in their daily work to create a better bottom line for their organizations.

Because I have gotten most of my experience from working with the Extended DISC model, this will be the model that I will use for examples during the book. I will refer to other DISC models once in a while to emphasize the differences. Please read more about this in the chapter regarding the major differences between the different models. In general, I will refer to "the DISC model," meaning the Extended DISC model.

This book is a brief introduction to the DISC model as well as an introduction to a variety of subjects, all of which are followed by examples.

Ethics

When choosing to work with an analysis tool in cooperation with people and organizations it is important to take ethical reflections into consideration. Depending on "how deeply we work," there may be different reflections. In the case of DISC models, I am talking about behavior and motivation, and not personality, values, or intelligence. You may come into contact with personality traits but only in the feedback session with the person who has filled in the questionnaire of the given behavioral analysis tool.

It is important to respect that the behavioral model can be used as a key to a discussion where personality, intelligence, and other aspects might emerge. The result of a computer-generated report can be a jumping off point for a conversation instead of a perfect picture of the one and only truth regarding a person's behavior. It can also provide an understanding of strengths, potential development, motivation, use of energy, and reasons behind procrastination in certain situations.

In Denmark, and much of the European countries within the EU, governments and psychologist and psychiatrist professional organizations place demands on the tools in use. These demands deal with validation of the tool, among other things.

When choosing which analysis or test to apply, it is important to make sure that the tool has been validated according to your country's psychological association's rules and demands. Your provider should openly and willingly show you the necessary documentations when asked. If not, choose another test or provider.

When working with personal tests and analysis it is important to consider your role and what kind of professional education and training that you have. If you are an educated psychologist or psychiatrist, you are trained to deal with people with mental health issues; the rest of us should not try to act as such professionals. The risks are too high. Know your limits, so you don't (accidentally) hurt people.

The report that computer based systems can give is a snapshot of the moment. So it is important to consider the situation the person being assessed is in. Some DISC models provide information on how valid the single result is. This is valuable information. If the result has a high validity, the result is more likely to be similar to the person in focus' view of him-/herself. And if the result has low validity, the result is likely to be different from the person in focus' view and may be completely wrong. This is why a result should never stand on its own. It is important to make sure that the person in focus and the report agree on the description.

In the next section, I will describe the theories behind the DISC model including work by Jung and later adapted by Sappinen for use in the workplace.

Jung – who was he?

Jung was a psychiatrist and psychotherapist (1875-1961) from Switzerland who founded analytical psychology. First, he worked together with the father of psychoanalysis, Sigmund Freud, but they had disagreements regarding basic topics, which made them part ways and not work together anymore.

Jung proposed and developed the concepts of the collective unconscious, archetypes, and extroversion and introversion. He was also interested in behavior and described 4 basic behavioral types:

* Sensing
* Intuition
* Thinking
* Feeling

Two of the types (sensing and intuition) regard the way the individual is gathering information. And they do it in very different ways. Actually, they do it in ways completely opposite to each other. This is the reason why there are often misunderstandings between perception and intuition when people are communicating and cooperating.

Sensing ⟵——————————⟶ Intuition

Sensing type

Sensing types are accurate and fact oriented. They take their time to find enough data and ensure that the data is correct and sufficiently detailed. After the data has been found, it needs to be organized in patterns - not necessarily generally known patterns. It will often be the individual's own created patterns and system that are used at this stage. The sensing types have high demands for quality. This will make them check and check again. It might seem as though they will never finish working with a task, but they will say there is always room for improvement.

The sensing type

* doesn't like new problems unless there is a standard way of solving them
* likes to do things in a certain approved way
* likes to use what has been learned instead of learning something new
* works steadily and knows how long it will take to solve a task
* gets there step by step
* is patient regarding routines and details
* will be impatient if the details get too complicated
* doesn't easily get inspired, and when it happens he is a bit skeptical towards it
* rarely makes factual mistakes
* is often good at precision work

The focus of the sensing type is facts and because of this, they can seem withdrawn, slow, and cold to opposite types.

Intuitive type

Intuitive types are quite the opposite of the sensing type. They seem to get information out of the blue. It is like they get a glimpse of insight and cannot tell how or why this information has come to them. The intuitive types will be interested in how the information fits into the big picture rather than checking details. This glimpse of insight appears, and less than a second later the intuitive types are ready to move on to a decision.

You might say that intuitive types like information for what it might be used for, whereas sensing types like information for the sake of information.

The intuitive type

* loves to solve new problems
* hates routines and any kind of repetition
* is more keen on learning something new rather than using it
* works at different paces, sometimes with high energy and sometimes with low
* gets to the results quickly
* hates details
* is impatient regarding complex matters
* follows inspiration and ideas, for good or bad
* often makes factual mistakes
* doesn't like to spend time on precision

The following description of the remaining types (thinking and feeling) will focus on how the types make decisions.

Thinking

Feeling

Thinking type

Thinking types are analytic. They will do calculations, which will be checked to ensure the quality of the work. The decision itself will be made after analysis in an objective way.

The thinking type

* can be firm
* can hurt others without knowing it
* likes to analyze and put things into logical order
* copes without any kind of harmony surrounding him
* wants to be treated fairly
* is the most analytic of the types
* reacts to others' thoughts
* focuses on the case when he makes decisions and will often be too little focused on others' wishes and needs
* gives reprimands or sacks people if necessary

Feeling type

Feeling types are not objective. On the contrary, they are subjective. They will weigh pros and cons against their personal values and principles. This means that even though feeling types all make the decision in a similar way, the decision may vary a lot from individual to individual. Feeling types are generally people-oriented and tend to see how they can protect the people in their group or family. They don't like to hurt others, and because of this, they will try to avoid conflicts of any kind.

The feeling type

* pays attention to others and their feelings
* is often open
* is people-oriented and reacts to others' values
* doesn't like to bring bad news
* needs to be praised now and then
* likes to please others, even if it really isn't important
* likes harmony because conflicts influence efficiency in a bad way
* will often let decisions be influenced by what others like or not

You can read more about Jung's theory in his book *The Psychological Types*. This is the theory that the Extended DISC was built upon by Jukka Sappinen back in 1994. But there are some other DISC models that are built on the theory of William Moulton Marston as he described it in the book *Behavior of Normal People*.

The DISC model

When Jukka Sappinen created the Extended DISC, he built on the different types outlined by Jung and developed four new basic styles specifically for application to employees in the workplace:

Dominance, Influence, Submissive, and Compliance

The dominant styles are competitive, aggressive, decisive, and result-oriented. They prefer to move fast, take risks, and get things done now.

Dominant styles also like to be in charge, in control, and to have the power. They like change and challenges – others might even say that they like change for the sake of change.

The dominant styles can also be impatient, overbearing, and even rude. They are often not very good listeners and are prone to make snap decisions. Others may perceive dominant styles as somewhat self-centered, demanding, blunt, and overly aggressive.

The influential styles are talkative, sociable, optimistic, and lively. They are people-oriented, spontaneous, energetic, and enthusiastic. Influential styles tend to be positive and good at influencing others. They can also be inattentive to details, overly talkative, and emotional. They may over-promise because they are so optimistic and are eager to be popular. Others may perceive intuitive styles as somewhat careless, impulsive, and lacking follow up.

Submissive styles are calm, helpful, patient, modest, and laid back. They are eager to help, loyal, and often make excellent team players. Submissive styles tend to be patient listeners, trustworthy, and balanced between tasks and people. They are very persistent.

Submissive styles need stability and security, and, therefore, need help with change. They may be too willing to pitch in and at times are taken advantage of. Others may perceive Submissive styles as too slow, stuck in the status quo, indecisive, stubborn, and even quietly resentful.

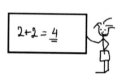

The compliance styles are precise, logical, matter-of-fact, analytical, and careful. They need data, information, and analysis. They are focused on tasks and ensure things get done correctly. Compliance styles tend to produce high quality work.

Compliance styles may also focus too much on the details, becoming nitpicky and slow, and losing the big picture. At times they get lost in the analysis, focusing too much on the trees and not the forest. Others may perceive compliance styles as too critical, distant, pessimistic, and even cold.

These words are brief introductions to the four basic styles. Throughout this book I will gradually provide more and more words to describe the styles including how they communicate, how they act under pressure, how they cooperate with others and more.

Notice that there are differences in description of the four basic types if you compare different DISC models. Some will, for example, have introversion and extroversion incorporated into the types and others do not. The Extended DISC doesn't measure types of introversion and extroversion.

Although these are the four basic styles, the Extended DISC model is so much more than this because the styles can be combined and provide 40 combination styles. And if you go even further into the model and do analysis, the Extended DISC "generator" can provide more than 1 million different profiles depending on the weight of the different styles in the precise profile.

If we list the 40 basic combinations it will look like this:

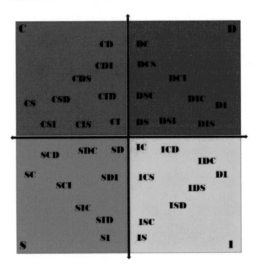

Throughout this book, when I refer to D types, I types, and so on, ALWAYS remember that these are just the basic types and you will meet so much more variety when you look at people around you.

Another thing to remember is that this is only measuring behavior and motivation. The Extended DISC is not a full description of a person - not how intelligent a person is, not what kind of skills a person has, nothing regarding values, ethics, experience, knowledge, or personality traits.

Saying this, I will sometimes tend to say that the styles are this or that because words are limiting when trying to explain behavior and motivation.

14

Natural and adjusted behavior

When discussing behavior in the DISC context there are two basic types:

* natural behavior
* adjusted behavior

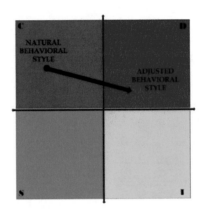

The natural behavior is the behavior that comes naturally to us and is totally connected with our basic or true motivation.

This natural behavior doesn't cost much energy to a person, which is why this behavior will be very visible when people are under pressure. When we are under pressure, we do not have enough energy to adjust our behavior.

When under pressure, we may not be able to see our behavior clearly – others will most likely will. When we are under pressure, our natural behavior will often be more visible and intensified.

Remember that motivation is not always about what we actually do, but what we can obtain from doing so.

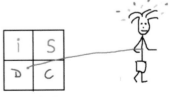

Adjusted behavior can appear in any situation, depending on what we want to achieve. Do we want to be as others expect? To obtain a certain goal?

Because of this, you may compare the adjusted behavior to acting out a role. This will cost more or less energy, depending on how far from your natural behavior you have to move.

Imagine that you have a rubber band attached to your back. This band is anchored where your natural behavior is placed on the map. When you adjust your behavior you move away from your natural behavior. The further away from your natural behavior (your anchor) that you move, the tighter the rubber band will get. When you move far away from the natural behavior (the anchor) the band will try to pull you back to the natural behavior. It will therefore cost quite a lot of energy to keep on adjusting.

Because of this, we can only carry out a major adjustment for a short time. And the effort will cost a lot of energy. We will have to go back to our natural behavior and maybe even go to sleep or do other things that will bring energy back to us.

When we face a task that we know from experience will demand a big adjustment from us, we may be prone to take care of other tasks (procrastinate) to avoid this demanding task. Some will even ignore the task for a while – hoping it will solve it self or go away.

Try to think of the last time you felt like drinking coffee, chatting with your colleagues, cleaning your desk, or going to the archive with loads of materials before working with this particular task? What kind of behavior will this task demand from you? That you work creatively and think of brand new solutions? Or that you work methodically and systematically? Or something completely different? When you have found this task, you will know something very important about yourself - your motivation and your natural behavior.

Because adjustment costs energy, and sometimes a lot of energy, we are not able to adjust our behavior all the time. So we (consciously or subconsciously?) choose when we do so. Some claim that we are not able to adjust our behavior more than 10-14% of the time. Others say that we can manage to do so for nearly 20% of the time.

Look at yourself, and when you have identified your natural behavior, try to think about how often you adjust the behavior.

Some DISC systems work with a concept called Job behavior. I consider this type of behavior as a combination of natural and adjusted behavior. And in the light of the brief discussion regarding adjusted and natural behavior, it must consist of 80% or more natural behavior and 20% or less adjusted behavior.

If job behavior should be something completely different than your natural behavior it will mean that you are adjusting on a major scale. This means you will be using a huge amount of energy to do so. Or from another perspective, you would have to leave your natural behavior in the wardrobe when go to work. Why anyone would do this doesn't make any sense to me.

Faithful or not?

- to your natural behavior.

One could argue that when we are adjusting our behavior we are unfaithful to our natural self. But could there be another perspective to this? Yes. There can be a number of reasons for why we choose to adjust our behavior instead doing what is natural to us.

All of our lives we are under influence of different people: our parents, siblings, teachers, trainers, managers, colleagues, friends, and so on. Some of these people will have demands of us, and many of us will find life easier if we do as these people want us to do, even if it is not according to our natural behavior.

Sometimes we will adjust our behavior to obtain something that we think will benefit us. For example, if we want a raise in monthly salary, we will go to our manager to have a discussion where we present our demands and reasons. But if we know that our manager's behavioral style is in a certain way – say D – we could adjust our behavior to resemble his behavior to make it easier for him to recognize what we want from him and to give us the result we want.

Even changes in society and culture or teams can make us adjust our behavior. In this modern world, it is important to be visible – whether you like it or not. But to people who don't have the very extroverted behavioral style, this can be anxiety provoking. To be a part of a team, some will adjust their behavior when they are together with the other team members. This can be hard to do, especially if you have to make a big adjustment. Then, you will use a lot of energy to so, and you will need to withdraw after a relatively short time to gain new energy.

If you are a lonely wolf on the team - meaning that you are the only one with your type of profile, and the rest of team have almost opposite profiles - you might feel the need to howl with the others in order to become and stay a part of the team.

Or it could be that you have an idol who you want to be like. You make adjustments to your behavior to be more like them.

These situations are quite common for all of us, and we do all adjust. As long as we know when we do so and why we do so, there are no big problems doing so. The problems with adjusting our behavior will arise if we don't acknowledge that we do so, that we think our natural behavior is different from what it is. Then we can get ourselves into trouble with pressure, stress, or even depression.

Characteristics and Areas for Development in the Four Types

Again, when you do the things the way you like to do them or do the things you like to do, it will cost you very little energy. It may even give you energy. We can say that you most often will find your strengths where you are truly motivated. This is not the kind of motivation that comes from wanting to satisfy others, like when we try to do as our parent, spouse, teacher, etc. wants us do or as we think they expect us to do. This motivation or behavior is actually mostly an adjusted motivation or behavior.

We have to look at true motivation, the behavior that truly is natural to us.

Sometimes we have worked with ourselves and done this work so well that we have changed the way we automatically behave. But this is still not a natural behavior or motivation to us. We do this now because we want to obtain a certain goal or to avoid certain difficulties.

If you find yourself under pressure, you will most likely return to your old behavior, which is your true natural behavior. Because when we are under pressure, we do not have the energy to be aware of adjusting our behavior.

All of the profiles have their own unique strengths.

Now let us take another look at each type.

Description of the D type:

Characteristics:
* Competing
* Initiating
* Pushy
* Busy
* Has many projects
* Demanding
* Direct
* Adventurous
* Goal- and future-oriented

Strengths:
* Re-organizes
* Creates changes
* Gets new ideas
* Pioneer

Communication:
* Direct and bold
* Talks more than listens
* Provides information without explanations
* Own ideas are communicated as facts that need no further discussion

Is motivated by:
* Victory
* Changes and variation
* Independence
* Possibility of reacting fast
* Clear measurable goals
* People who take initiative

<u>Areas for development:</u>

* Listen more
* Analyze more thoroughly
* Accept and create continuity
* Sell changes
* Remember people
* Ask instead of giving orders
* Stop creating pressure

People?
What do you mean?

We will often say that the D types don't focus on quality, details, or people – but it's not quite true. It really depends on what the D type's goals, values, and knowledge are.

If a D type is rewarded when his staff scores a high level in the yearly climate survey in the company, he will put a great effort into making the people thrive. Some D types have learned that it is rarely possible to achieve all goals by themselves. They need others with different skills to get there. And they might have learned to motivate and inspire others – not because they like to do so, but because it will help them get what they really want: To be the winner.

Some D types can see that they need assistance to get to the goal, but they haven't found out how to get it. So they give orders and bully people into solving the tasks. This often results in poor solutions and people leaving the project before completion.

Description of the I style

<u>Characteristics:</u>
* Communicative
* Social
* Pleasant
* Active
* Motivating
* Inspiring
* Enterprising
* Sociable
* Change-seeking
* Emotional

<u>Strengths:</u>
* Keeps a positive atmosphere
* Invites everyone to participate
* Gets people to hang on
* Encourages, motivates, and inspires

<u>Is motivated by:</u>
* Friendly atmosphere
* Exchange of ideas and thoughts
* Spontaneity
* Belonging to the team
* Change of place and new situations

<u>Communication:</u>
* Selling and inspiring style
* Talks a lot
* Avoids details
* Talks about possibilities
* Good at positive feedback

<u>Areas for development:</u>
* React more quickly at signs of danger
* Learn to make unpleasant decisions
* Make small changes
* Focus less on the good mood
* Talk about the unpleasant stuff, too

23

Some will see the I type as foolish and unable to do serious work. I recommend that you watch out for this assumption. The I type can be very focused and rather detail-orientated IF they can see that they will be popular and get recognized by managers and other important persons. It is not the focus that motivates them, but what they can achieve from the focus.

And many I types have learned that they need structure to make sure they will do as promised – again this will get them the praise they need. This means they often are very good at using all kinds of devises to their aid, like smart phones with calendars, which are always accessible.

Description of the S style

Characteristics:
* Considerate
* Stable
* Systematic
* Thorough
* Modest
* Good listener
* Has empathy

Strengths:
* Keeps promises
* Listens to all instructions
* Likes routines, which can improve clarity
* Doesn't change for the sake of change
* Team player

Communication:
* Prefers to talk one-on-one
* Listens, nods, answers when asked
* Calm
* Prefers to talk about things he knows about

Is motivated by:
* Stability and security
* Honesty
* Straightforwardness
* Belonging to the group – being with people he knows
* Possibility to think about things (especially before making a decision)
* Systematic surroundings
* Credibility

Areas for development:
* Ask when in doubt
* Make bigger changes
* Don't get stuck in routines
* Demand more
* Make bigger and more critical decisions
* React fast

I stick to what I know!!

We often say that the S type doesn't like changes and that is more or less correct. But it depends. If we expect the S type to initiate big changes, we are up for disappointment. But, if we present the need to change along with the reason why we should change, it will be much easier for the S type to come on board.

The best scenario would be to present the need for change and let the S type work out how this change should be conducted. Don't expect to get the answer straight away. He will need to think about it and sleep on it before he will present his solution. And when this change, and the way it should be done, has been decided, the S type will have a far better ownership of this change process. He will work hard all the way till the end of it (which is much more than we can expect from some of the other types).

Description of the C style

Characteristics:
* Precise
* Logical
* Sensible
* Modest
* Fact oriented
* Careful

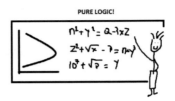

Strengths:
* Finds errors and mistakes
* Guarantees good quality
* Thorough and detail-oriented
* Systematic
* No emotions in decisions – objective
* Careful in a natural way

Is motivated by:
* Possibility to specialize
* Concentration and focus on the facts
* High quality
* Thoroughness
* Competent colleagues
  Well-structured tasks

Communication:
* Cautious
* Withdrawn
* Hesitant, but will answer when asked as the specialist

Areas for development:
* Remember people – they need to be motivated and inspired
* Don't get stuck in the details
* Don't isolate yourself
* Make decisions based on less details

I have heard many people say that the C type is so orderly. But I have met quite a few C types who were SO messy! The C type likes systems and order where he has his interest. Everywhere else, it doesn't matter so much. Think about the professor, the auditor, the lawyer, and their offices. Some of them are full of piles of paper and folders. It seems impossible to find anything in this mess. But ask him for a specific file and 1-2-3 he has picked it out of the heaps.

You can discover that the C type has some vital information to solve the task the team is working on. But he doesn't always come forward with it. When you confront him why he didn't come up with this information, he might say: You didn't ask for it.

What will provide and drain energy for each of the four basic types?

When we do things in a way that suits our basic motivation we can almost feel as if we get energy from it – even though we work rather hard. There is a big difference in what will give the C type energy and what will give the I type energy. Actually, the C type will most likely lose energy when he has to work in the way the I style prefers. Let us check out some examples:

The D style gets energy when he gets the sense of competition. In situations where he can be the winner, he will feel wonderful. The chance of being influential, capable of making risky decisions, or at least deciding will also influence his motivation. If he gets the results he sat out to get or if others consider him a first mover or pioneer, it will do well for his general motivation.

If he, on the other hand, has to work with a task that has a larger degree of routines, projects, or processes that move slow or tasks that demand keeping strictly to the rules, he will be bored and lose motivation.

I hate all of those rules!

When people stand up and try to counteract changes, he will get tired. When there are no goals or objectives, or there are emotional discussions and decisions, the same will happen.

The I type will be more motivated if he can be with others, working together or just having them around him working while he is working. The activity and good mood will rub off on him and make him even more creative and full of ideas that he can share and discuss with someone else. I types like very much to become the winner because the winner will be recognized and praised, which he loves. But, it is important to notice that he doesn't want to be the winner at any cost! If it is at the expense of popularity, he prefers not to win. The feeling of freedom and flexibility and possibility to meet new people – this will give him lots of energy.

Home alone

And like the D type, the I type doesn't like to work with anything that reminds him of routines. It makes him lose even more energy if the tasks have to be solved at a high degree of detail, structure, and strict rules.

When the discussions turn to a purely professional level, the I type will often be seen checking his smart phone. He will not do this every time the discussion gets professional; he will be participating if he can see that he will gain popularity from this.   You can always recognize an I type who has been on his own way too long: He will be talking, talking, talking.

The S type is, like the I type, motivated when he is together with other people, along with the positive atmosphere where things can grow in a stable environment. He also likes to be recognized and feel that he belongs to the team. But the S type prefers to be able to work steadily and undisturbed. And he gets more energy when he can help and support others and receive the same for himself without asking for it.

To say "no" or to ask for help are two things that drag the energy from the S type and make him lose his motivation.

So good to be part of the team

Often, he will walk around talking to himself (maybe inside his head) about how to solve the challenge that it is to say no to somebody before actually doing so in real life.

The S type doesn't like to be the one who starts on the new task. He will prefer to have objectives and a framework settled before he begins. If the S type finds himself in an environment where people talk and act disloyally, it will make him lose his motivation and energy.

The C type will get more energy and feel more motivated if he is left to himself to solve tasks at his own pace and quality, especially if he feels he has enough time to work thoroughly and in a very professional way. This means that the C type typically thrives best in a highly professional work environment with firm structures and systems.

The C type doesn't find emotional discussions worth spending energy on. It doesn't really make any sense to him. So, if he is forced into such a discussion, he will not be motivated or gain any energy.

Feels good to be among peers

The same thing will happen if we keep disturbing him when he is working or if the deadlines are narrow or change for the worse. He hates delivering unfinished solutions, and he will get the feeling that he does deliver unfinished products if he hasn't had enough time to work thoroughly and check the quality.

Reaction when under pressure

Everyone feels under pressure from time to time. What creates pressure for each of us is very different and how we react under pressure is also very different. What I can say is that we most likely live out our natural behavior to the fullest when under pressure. Check the lists below, and observe the difference between behaviors when each style is in balance and when under pressure.

D style in balance	D style under pressure
* Gives brief instructions	* Commands
* Initiates changes and new projects	* Creates pressure in the organization with constant changes and new decisions
* Decisive	
* Clear demands	* Own opinion is enforced as fact
* Works with focus on the goal	* Intolerant
* Fact oriented	* Arrogant
* Demanding	* Ruthless
* Strong willpower	* Officious
* Energetic	* Impatient
* Resolute	* Rude
* Competing	* Controls others' achievements

WORK HARDER!

31

I style in balance	I style under pressure
* Convinces	* Exaggerates
* Outgoing	* Overwrought
* Enthusiastic	* Frivolous
* Talks a lot	* Speaks loudly
* Optimistic	* Unstructured
* Brings up new ideas	* Indiscreet
* Spontaneous	* Superficial at work
* Dynamic	* Works when others work
* Creates new contacts	* Jumps hectically from task to task without getting anything done

S style in balance	S style under pressure
* Considerate	* Stubborn
* Careful	* Cautious
* Friendly	* Indecisive
* Loyal	* Elusive
* Attentive	* Withdrawn
* Understanding	* Implacable
* Calm	* Oversensitive
* Discreet	* Waits
* Works constantly until the work is done	* Gives up if there is resistance
* Makes sure everyone is heard	* Avoids unpleasant subjects

C style in balance	C style under pressure
* Exact	* Cold
* Systematic	* Isolates
* Analyzes	* Punctilious
* Investigates	* Awkward
* Sensible	* Petty
* Methodical	* Indecisive
* Disciplined	* Not receptive to others' arguments
* Stable	* Aggressive when met with criticism or errors of others
* Has precise arguments	
* Objective	

Ready for re-re-re-check!

And why do we get under pressure?

When our basic needs and motivation aren't met we often experience pressure to some degree. If this keeps on for a longer period, then the pressure will mount up and we will see the behavior under pressure as described above. Below is a list of what puts each style under pressure.

The C style	The D style
* Lack of time to solve tasks * Lack of control that the solution is of sufficient quality * Feeling of delivering something half finished * Narrow deadlines * Making emotional decisions	* Working in groups * Lack of goals * When the D style's change initiative is blocked * Lack of results * Making emotional decisions

The S style	The I style
* Lack of recognition from the manager * Unclear job descriptions * Initiating new tasks on his own * Great changes (especially if there are no arguments regarding why or if the arguments conflict with the values and principles of the S style)	* Working alone * Being alone for a long period * Negative atmosphere * Silence * Lack of recognition from the manager * Narrow deadlines for a task with many details

But, of course, there can be many other reasons that will create pressure.

Help the poor fellow

Is there any way we can help the poor fellow when he is under pressure – and thereby help ourselves? Yes. How? Give him the surroundings and conditions he needs to be balanced.

The D style will be more in balance if they are allowed to compete and are able to win the competition, create changes, and make difficult and risky decisions. Having influence on decisions or being the one who decides will contribute to this. The D style feels great if he is the pioneer, the first mover. Getting the results he wants – or more – will make him feel even better.

If we want to provide balance for the I style, we should give him possibilities to be together with other people – work together with them or just be (talk) with them. The I style will be happiest if the atmosphere is kept on a positive level which means that even competitions should be kept in a positive mood. Of course, the I style likes to win, but not at any cost. If it means loss of popularity, it will not be that interesting to be the winner. But the I style loves and thrives on recognition from the surroundings – and it is alright if it is loud. He loves to meet new people and talk about and create solutions with them. One could say that freedom and flexibility is the headline.

To be and work together with other people is also very motivating for the S style. This means he belongs to the team. He likes a positive atmosphere where agreements, values, and principles are respected. Like the I style, he likes to be recognized but in a completely different way: He prefers if it is one-to-one and more private. The S style likes work without interruptions (which will destroy the routines). He likes to help and support others – he also needs support himself but he finds it hard to ask for it.

The C style loves to dig into a task so that it will be solved thoroughly and will be a high quality solution. He likes to have the time to specialize in a specific subject. He loves to work in a very professional work environment where the colleagues have the same kind of professional interests and standards as himself. Firm and fixed structures and systems are the base of life itself, and if you disturb or don't respect the structures, you will be condemned. A C style might not like any structure or system you provide for him. He may want to create his own.

Decisions

When we talk about decisions we can dissect them into four steps:

* Information gathering
* Analysis and calculation
* Decision making
* Evaluating

The four basic behavioral styles handle these steps very differently as we will take a closer look at in the following section.

The D style spends very little time on gathering information, and therefore do not collect much information, only what he finds important. The analysis step is done quickly because there are not many facts to consider, and D styles do have clear goals. The evaluation step has a focus on whether the decision will get him where he wants – whether he will obtain the goal or not, or you could say the focus is on effectiveness and being the winner.

The I style will also use a brief time to gather information – details are not his favorite aspect of a task. The analysis step is done quickly, too, since his gut feeling helps him along the way. And then the decision can be made. The evaluation portion has a focus on whether the I style will be seen as the star since the I style's main focus is too be popular, get recognition, and stay away from negative vibes. So if it is not possible to be popular from this decision, it will be very hard for the I style to make it.

The S style spends more time on finding the information he thinks is important. He analyzes but often he lacks confidence in himself, so he will consult his surroundings to get advice and opinions. The larger the risk is that someone will get hurt, the more difficult it will be for the S style to make a decision. The evaluation will focus on securing that no one got hurt and explaining why this decision had to be made like this. The overall perspective for the S style is that everyone is heard and taken into consideration.

The C style gathers a lot of information, which is checked thoroughly before the deep analysis is started. The results are checked over and over again to ensure that everything is correct. Now, the C style is ready to make a decision. This part doesn't take a very long time because the data and the calculation have been checked. Evaluation has a focus on whether there should have been even more data available to the analyze – the worst case scenario is when he has forgotten some vital information. Generally, the focus of the C style is objectivity and analyzing. He believes that this is the only way to make decisions of supreme quality.

It is important to remember that these methodologies apply only when we have to make larger decisions and not when we have to decide what to eat for dinner and so on. They apply when we have invested more money, if we don't have experience or knowledge on a subject, or if making a decision is connected with significant risks.

If a C style or S style are to make decisions, including risky ones, it is not a big problem for them to do so swiftly and precisely if it is within their professional area. Think about the casualty room in the hospital. The doctors here have spent years training for each situation and can quickly assess the situation and make the right decision.

The C style will be challenged with his decision making if he can't handle all of the details or if the decision needed is regarding emotions.

S styles can also easily make quick decisions if they are within their professional area, even though they have a reputation for being indecisive or very hesitant decision makers. The S style will most likely be hesitant if people may be hurt or if the S style will be in conflict with his values or principles.

The D style will typically be challenged when it is about emotions – just like the C styles. But the D style will also be challenged if the decision demands a high degree of deep and thorough analysis.

The I style will most likely handle the emotional decisions quite easily – it is the opposite that will challenge him. And on top of this, the I style may make a decision and then other solutions will appear - then, they will make another, and another, and another. Also, unpleasant decisions or decisions that will make the I style unpopular will cause challenges too.

<u>Example:</u>

The company has to sack an employee in the sales department because of the need to save generally. But who should go?

D style: I have checked the sales for everyone in the department and the one who has the worst results in the last quarter will go. So, Jock, goodbye.

I style: I have checked the sales for everyone in the department. Jock did the poorest result of all last quarter. But he is always the one who is helping the others to get their job done. So I will get everyone in the department against me if I choose to sack him. Maybe I should choose André – he will easily find another job.

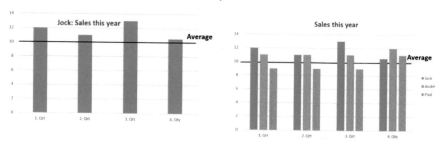

S style: I know we need to cut down. But everyone has been working so hard. It is not fair to sack anyone. I think that if we all have a reduction in our bonus and fees, no one will be sacked.

C style: I have checked the numbers for the last 12 months, calculated averages per month, and compared to single sales persons' sales month for month and much more. Some are very stable in their performances, and some are not. I know that Jock didn't do very well last quarter, but generally he is a top dog. So, all in all, it is Paul who has to leave us since his performance generally is below average.

Another example: The Smith family and the Johnson family have talked about buying a summer house in the countryside. Each family should own 50% of the house.

Dan S: I have already checked the market and found the perfect house for us. There is room for everyone and the price is good – especially if we haggle a little! Well, actually I have already contacted the owner, and we are very close to having a deal.

Imogen J: That sounds wonderful. Think about it! This summer we can enjoy the wonderful countryside. Yes, we might have to do some painting and so on. But if we help each other, it will be done swiftly!

Sarah S: Are you sure? Shouldn't we see some more houses before we decide? Just to be sure?

Charles J: You are so right, Sarah. We need to make a budget to be able to evaluate the cost for reparations and make checklists to see what we prioritize in a house before we even start looking at the houses.

Outdoors:				
	Paint	€		123,00
	Nails	€		50,00
	Timber	€		2.000,00
	Garden tiles	€		3.000,00
	Windows	€		2.500,00
Bathroom:				
	Toilet	€		175,00
	Sink	€		250,00
	Tiles	€		500,00
	Shower	€		500,00
	Drain	€		125,00
	Plumbing	€		4.500,00
Kitchen:				
	Table	€		100,00
	Cabinets	€		300,00
	Draws	€		300,00
	Stove	€		350,00
	Fridge	€		350,00
	Freezer	€		350,00
Livingroom:				
	Sofa	€		700,00
	Table	€		900,00
	Coffeetable	€		200,00
	Paint	€		200,00
	Floor	€		620,00
SUM:		€ 18.093,00		

Imogen J: Oh, I think Dan has it under control. I am sure it can be done. I do look forward to enjoying the countryside in summer sun.

Dan S: Argh! Come on! It is just a summer house. We don't need checklists! Don't make it so complicated!

Sarah: But there are so many things that might go wrong. Hidden errors and so...

Dan S: This is why we should buy cheap. Then we can demolish and build something new and fancy!

Sarah S: But then there will be no spirit or soul in the house. And how will we be able to have it all done before summer?

Charles J: I refuse to throw myself and my money into a project that is so badly planed. No details at all. No budgets! I demand thoughtful decisions!

Imogen J: Oh Charles, don't be so boring! Think more positively!!

But, in general, we can say the four styles will try to make decisions in a way that is coherent with their basic behavioral style. That means

D styles will try to look bold, brave, decisive, adventurous, as the winner and so on.

I styles love to look popular, as winners (but not at all cost like the D) so they will have the recognition they thrive for.

S styles hope that their decisions will help keep the status quo, ensuring all are heard and taken into consideration.

C styles' motivation comes from the wish to make objective decisions based on a set of information that is well worked through.

A lot of people experience, at some point of their life, the buying of real estate – a house or an apartment. And to most people, this is a pretty big decision, so in this situation, the basic preferences will most likely step forward.

Checklist

alhjafoe	✓
alhjafoe	✓
alhjafoe	
alhjafoe	
alhjafoe	✓
alhjafoe	
alhjafoe	✓
kjhfa	
afhlie	✓
hljasdf	
alhjafoe	✓
hlaf	
lajfs	✓
kjalhf	
wruly	
albf	✓
alhjafoe	
jhlkasdf	NOW!
alhjafoe	
kjhafp	
alhjafoe	NOW!
jafdh	
uwpfh	
lkajdf	
blkaf	
ahfua4	
qupwfa	
oiuwqyr	
wqrhe	

The C styles will typically make a list of demands which are almost mandatory. For example, regarding location, number of rooms, how much reparation is needed. All properties will be compared to these demands. The more pressure the C styles experience, the more rigidly they will stick to their demands and thereby make the decision even harder.

The S styles will also make lists of demands – just like the C styles. But they are more likely not stick to them as objectively as the C styles. They will see other positive or negative things about each property, and this will make it harder to decide. Then they will get help and advice from experts and friends. But not just one. No, everyone needs to give their opinion which, again, will muddy the picture and make it harder for them to decide.

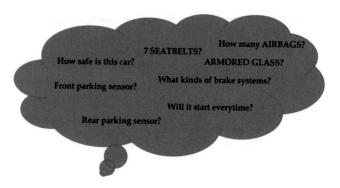

The I styles can make a list of demands but often they will fall in love with a property and choose to neglect the flaws and errors. And then they are left with huge extra bills for reparations....

The D styles love to make fast decisions, which makes them able to move on to something new. This means they easily miss critical issues. But different from the I styles, the D styles will then try to overturn the decision or try to negotiate a refund or get the price down so they again will look as the winner.

Communication and cooperation between the four basic styles

When two or more people need to cooperate, for example, regarding the completion of a task, communication is needed. And as you will see, the four basic behavioral styles prefer to communicate with a different focus and in different ways. Notice that I will only look at the spoken and written communication, not the non-verbal part of communication.

D styles don't use an abundance of words. They like to communicate, both in writing and the spoken word, in brief, using precise and concise words. If you see an email from a D style you will properly find a few bullet points and nothing more. If you write an email that contains more than one question to a D style, do not be surprised if you only receive an answer to one of them.

I styles just love to talk. And they are very good at it. In general, I styles are good at telling stories. By stories I don't mean something they invent. No, I mean when they have to tell somebody about a subject, they paint a picture to tell you about it. They do it in an inspiring way, so inspiring that even boring topics find a new life. The I style's habit of seeing only the positive side of things is also what they will be communicating. So, it might not be a good idea to let an I style deliver sad news since they will try avoid the unpleasantness. The result could be that the audience could get the wrong message.

In general, I styles will prefer to talk about things. Think of an exam. If it is oral, the I styles will often be better off than the rest of the styles because they are good at using words. Of course, they can do this in writing, but it often works better for them when talking to an audience.

The S styles don't like as big an audience as the I styles. Actually, they prefer one-to-one communication or communication within small groups. The spoken word is number one, and they prefer to be face-to-face – this doesn't matter to C styles and D styles to the same degree because their focus is not on people but on facts.

Of course, S styles can be great teachers – a role where the S style is forced to address a larger audience. To do this, they will need time to prepare and maybe even do a pre-run of the lecture or have a senior colleague check the facts and methods to be sure everything is perfect.

One thing S styles definitely have a challenge in communicating is the little word: NO. As in:

* no, I haven't got the time to solve this task
* no, I haven't got the skills to do this task
* no, I don't want this position in the team
* and so on...

Most often, it is because the S styles are afraid to hurt people if they say no or decline an offer. If it's the boss who will be receiving the no, it might be fear of losing his job or interesting tasks.

C styles are quite opposite from the I styles. If you ask a C style to stand up and talk about his ideas, analysis, or conclusion, he will properly seem shy and very modest. He might even refuse to stand up in front of the audience if you don't give him time to prepare his speech. Actually, C styles can be fantastic lecturers if they have the time to prepare themselves and have the time to gain experience. Often, they will prepare. They will have material for hours of teaching just to be on the podium for 1 hour. And they will have pre-run their lecture to check if the time table fits.

C styles will, in general, prefer a written correspondence. Think about the emails you get. If you get emails from a C style they will often be long, with lots of details, and may include links to where you can find additional documentation. And you can be pretty sure if this correspondence has been going on for some time, the original email and all of the following emails will be found in the end of this mail. Much easier than having to save a lot of emails – just save one, and you have them all.

Cooperation

The four basic styles must, of course, cooperate in a great deal of situations: On the job, in the family, in the community, in the sports club, and so on. But how will this work? They are rather different in the way they are motivated, preference for working alone or not, and how they communicate. But, the styles have two things in common with other styles, which will make it easier for them to cooperate. Look at this figure:

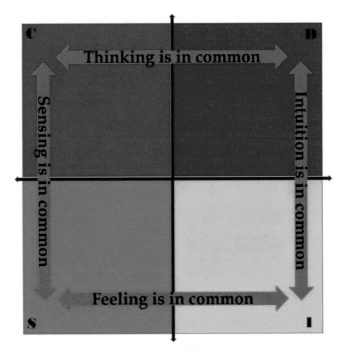

Functional cooperation involves well-functioning communication. But how do we obtain that when we have four basic behavioral styles who are very different? And does it get any better when we include all the possible combinations? Remember that if we combine 2 and 3 styles plus the 4 basic styles we will get 40 options. Here come a few tips for you to make it easier. First we will take a look at who easily works together and who finds it difficult.

Who gets along?

<u>The D style and the I style</u>   **D ≠ I**

- Have the intuitive part in common. They gather information in the same way: looking at the big picture without any details, seeing how things fit into the big plan, and finding opportunities. And, this happens pretty fast. So, they have the speed in common.

But when it comes to making decisions, they stop agreeing. The D style is controlled by thinking – it is logical, analytical. The I style is controlled by feeling – it is assessing and comparing to values and principles. Here is the basis for conflicts.

The I style thinks the D style is hard, insensitive, and ignores other people. From I's perspective this is just bad. D styles give orders, put pressure on others, don't listen, and are far too serious.

The D style thinks the I style is silly, unserious, doesn't keep focused long enough, and isn't ambitious enough. The I style is far too emotional and often too unproductive for the D style. And they talk way too much!!

<u>The I style and the S style</u>   I ≠ S

- Have the way they make decisions in common – with the use of feeling. But, they collect the needed information in very different ways. The I style uses intuition. The S style, on the contrary, uses the 5 senses – hearing, smelling, tasting, touching, and seeing. Because of this, the S style gets factual information that is checked, structured, and fitted into the existing systems. His is a bit slower of a way to get information than intuition.

And this difference provides the basis for conflicts.
The I style thinks that the S style is too cautious, slow to get started, and gets stuck in the routines and traditions. He is not ready to bend rules

even if it will help in getting the best resolution of the task.

The S style finds the I style to be flighty and unpredictable because he changes his mind all the time. The I style wants changes all the time (which the S style doesn't), and the I style thinks more of himself than of the people that surround him – opposite the S style who thinks of others and then, maybe, himself.

But they do agree on that focus on people, emotions, and making decisions on gut feeling.

The S and the C style   S ≠ C

- Have the way of getting information in common: the use of sensing. But, they decide in different ways. The S style will use feeling, and the C style will use thinking.

The S style will look at the C style as very hard, unyielding, cold, unapproachable, rigid, categorical, and insensitive. To the S style, the C style thinks far too little about other people and their feelings.

And the C style consider the S style too soft, emotional, insecure, which means he always has to ask everyone about their opinion when decisions are needed.

The C and the D style   D ≠ C

- Have the way they make decisions in common: thinking. This means they agree that decisions have to be made through analysis and deliberate thinking. Objectivity is king.

But the D style gets his information from intuition and the C style his from sensing. This gives the D style the view that the C style is slow, indecisive, and far too thorough to be efficient. According to the D style, the C style's focus on details is killing any sense of progress and development – even though the C styles are practical to have on the team to ensure the necessary quality.

The C style sees the D style as sloppy, too loud, and dominant. He is too fast when he makes decisions on a far too thin of a basis. He makes changes just to make changes even if there really isn't a need for it.

Who doesn't get along?

<u>The I and the C style</u>   I ≠ C

- Do not agree on anything. At all. They get information differently. and they decide differently. Here, there is a good basis for conflict....

The C style finds the I style to be sloppy and too emotional. He talks too much and about all kinds of stuff. He changes subject constantly, and it gets more and more irrelevant. He is unfocused and never seems to get anything finished. What a waste of time!

The I style, on the other hand, thinks that the C style is cold and unyielding, almost impersonal. He is so dry and full of dust. He never goes anywhere because it takes him too long to make up his mind to go. And he is so serious that all the fun vaporizes. What good is he for?

- Do not agree on anything, just like C and I.

The S style will see the D style as too dominant, shouting too loud. He makes constant changes, which is very disturbing to the S style, and he wants to decide without listening to anyone else or taking into concern anyone else.

The D style thinks, on the other hand, that the S style is slow and indecisive, emotional to the point of blubbering, and always seeing the dark side of matters. He is never game when it comes to a good idea or new development. He is retrogressive!

Communication summary

At first look it seems we will never get anyone to cooperate. But, it can be done if the four basic styles learn to know each other, for better or worse. And, naturally, it demands that everyone is open and tolerant toward the differences. A good place to start working on this is communication.

It demands that everyone is ready to sacrifice their own needs to get communication up and running. It is about everyone adjusting their communication to meet others more openly. How this will happen will be explained in the next section with examples. Remember that the phrases are meant as good advice and examples; they are not a precise recipe.

Some general advice regarding communication...

What you need to consider when you adjust your communication is more or less this:

* Do you need to speed up or slow down?
* How many details do you need to provide?
* Are you talking emotions or facts?
* Do you talk or write to people?

Below you will find a matrix to guide your communication. The way you use the matrix is like this:

* You locate your personal primary style
* Then you follow the column until you find the row that represents the communication partner's primary style

If I have S as my primary style and I need to talk to a C style, I will follow the S column to the lowest row and take into consideration the overlap and mismatch of our two styles.

	D	I	S	C
D				
I				
S				
C				

In the following example, the character's first names coincide with their primary style:

Dan needs some reports from his colleague Charlotte.

Dan: Charlotte, hand me the reports regarding last month's sales.
Charlotte: Here.
Dan looks at the report and finds this is not what he expected.
Dan: This is not the right report. This is only total numbers.
Charlotte: You didn't ask for anything but sales reports.
Dan: All right. I would like to have the report that shows what each salesperson sold last month!
Charlotte: Here.

India also needs reports from Charlotte:
India: Hi Charlotte. How are you doing?
Charlotte: OK.
India: How was your vacation?
Charlotte: Fine.

India: I was on a trip just this weekend with my boyfriend. Wonderful hotel. Lovely food. Spa. Massage. And the nature was so beautiful. We went walking on the beach and in the woods. Amazing. We should do that more often. You simply return with so much energy. Maybe we should have somebody coming here and giving us a backrub every now and then. Like every week. Your shoulders just ache after all this computer work. I am sure it would be good for everyone – including the company. Don't you think?
Charlotte: Well...

India: Yes! And then we wouldn't have that many sick days because of headaches! Oh well. I think I will go to Dan and suggest it to him. Hmm, why did I come to see you? Oh, yes, I need some reports from you.

Charlotte: Yes?

India: About the sales in last month...

Charlotte: Here.

Adjusting our behavior or communication?

We can walk through life without adapting or adjusting to our surroundings. With the risk of being misunderstood and get into a lot of conflicts if the surroundings don't respond in a positive way to our communication and behavior. And people will not respond positively if they keep to their preferences – especially if their preference is the opposite of yours. Then, we will only be able to have good communication with the ones who have a similar style as ourselves.

So, it is quite suitable to adjust our behavior and communication when we meet people with other styles. But how do we do it best?

Well, we have to try to do things in the same way as the person we are communicating with. So, if I am a D style and want to engage with an S style, I must try to do things in "an S way". This will cost a lot of energy to adjust this much, so I will only be able to do it for a short while or else I will be exhausted. If a D style has to talk to an I style, it will be much easier since they have in common that they gather information in the same fast way using intuition, as seen in the previous chapter.

When we make major adjustments it will not only cost us a lot of energy, but also we will often be less successful doing so because we will not be able to be truly genuine. You have properly experienced this when talking to somebody. There seems to be something wrong. Something undefinable. It will be most clear if you know the person and can tell that this is not his usual behavior or way of communicating. You might instinctively ask yourself what he is up to.

Let me give you an example: An S style wants to let someone know that he has over-stepped the limits, and the S style really wants to make it totally clear. So, he tries to be more like a D. It could look like this if it was a true D style argument: "You have stepped over the line. Stop doing that at once!"

But the S style will be likely to over-do the adjustment: "It is absolutely not okay that you do this! You are stepping over the line! I want you to stop immediately! You must stop it! Now! Because I am telling you to!"

Sometimes we need more or less of a certain behavior to get success. Let's take a look at what you can do to get more or less of the four different styles in your behavior and communication.

More D	Less D
Actions	Things to Consider
* Be more direct and demanding toward others * Accept new and different tasks more often * Use your authority in different situations * Make decisions faster – even when there are risks * Stick to your own decisions – even if they are not comfortable for other people * Participate more often in competitions with yourself or others * Be more powerful in your expression * Have more trust and confidence in yourself and your capabilities * Do more experiments and take initiative to make changes	* What will be the consequences of your actions or remarks? * What results can you get if you actively listen more to others and their thoughts, ideas, and experiences? * How can you be a winner by letting others win? * How will others react if you give them the reasons to your decisions? * What results can you achieve by participating in a group session instead of leading it? * How will your employees react if you give them more recognition when they have earned it? * What can you achieve if you use an appreciative tone when you communicate?

More I	Less I
Actions	Things to Consider
* Be the initiator more often to get in contact with others – even if you don't know them	* What positive consequences would it have for you if you were better at controlling your time?
* Involve others in the solution of the task so you do it together	* How will it strengthen you if you are more direct and firm in situations with conflicts?
* Tell more about yourself, your opinions, and thoughts	* What could you achieve by assessing the positive AND the negative sides of a case?
* Communicate more and not just in writing – also make speeches in meetings	* What results could you obtain if focused a bit more on the details?
* Use pictures and metaphors to inspire and motivate	* What would you win if you were better at keeping track of your time?
* Be constructive when giving feedback	* If you were more critical regarding your use of time in meetings, what could you obtain from doing so?
* Show recognition to others	
* Sell ideas and decisions	
* Initiate and participate in social activities	
* Participate in more group activities – both on the job and in private	

More S	Less S
Actions	Things to Consider
* Be more tolerant and patient with your surroundings * Sharpen your attention to others' needs * Show care for others' needs by helping them without being asked to do so * Be focused on continuity, principles, and routines * Work together with others * Have an easy and calm work pace towards the goal * Keep focus on rules, morals, and norms * Listen for a longer time and be an active listener * Listen more and talk less * Contribute to the creation of ownership for activities in the group	* What positive effects can changes have? * In which situations would it be appropriate to say no? * In which situations would it be appropriate to stand firmly in your own point of view? * How would it be if it was you who took initiative to create clarity in a difficult situation? * How can you handle challenges in way that will give you better feedback or a better return? * How can you carry out improvements so that your solutions get better and more efficient according to the visions and goal of the company?

More C	Less C
Actions	Things to Consider
* Be more focused on details and precision when solving tasks	* What positive effects could it have on your solution of tasks if you could think of more nuances than black and white?
* Be critical to facts, information, and solution models so errors are found and corrected	
* Use facts and analysis as your basis for decisions	* In which situations do others contribute positively to the solution?
* Stay neutral in situations with conflicts	* What can you learn from the fact that others solve the tasks in different ways than you?
* Consider solutions and decisions thoroughly using facts and analysis	* What can you do to give less critical feedback and more recognition to your employees and colleagues?
* Work independently	
* Make detailed plans before solving the task	* What would it mean if you took initiative to share your knowledge?
* Use logical arguments	
* Focus on quality instead of quantity	* How would it be to talk about other things than professional topics?
* Spend less time on the social when cooperating with colleagues	* What would it mean to you to make small mistakes?
* Work steadily and with a consistent level of quality	

Celebrity Examples

Why do authors choose to have very different characters in their movies and books? To create some dynamics. If you let opposite profiles meet, something is bound to happen. Since they communicate differently and do things differently there is a basis for conflict. The conflicts move the story. Now, I don't think about conflicts as wars but as an energy that will be able to move the story forward.

Let's look at an example: The TV series "Friends". Some of the basic roles are

* Monica
* Chandler
* Joey

These three have different behavioral styles according to the DISC theory:

* Monica – loves to be in control, having thorough and precise plans, order, and systems; she hates when others are not as organized and well-structured as herself.
* Chandler – doesn't like change very much, prefers to stay together and do things together. He hates conflicts even though he sometimes tumbles into them with Monica
* Joey – no system in anything, prepared to talk himself out of trouble, charm his way through life, seeking pleasure and acknowledgment. Since he is not very focused on details, he loses job after job.

Which gives the series a C, S, and I – a perfect opportunity for the writers to have some action.

Not all series are built on the four DISC behavioral styles on purpose but when you look into them, lots of them do fit with the model. Maybe not as the basic styles, but often quite clear combinations as ID, DC, SI, and so on. In this way the characters will be easier for the viewer to identify with themselves.

When you watch TV shows like American Idol, Britain's Got Talent, etc., you will notice that here itis often the judges who are representing the four basic styles. Take Simon Cowell, a bit dominant or what?

You could also observe world leaders and managers of international companies:

* Donald Trump (business man) – dominance
* Bill Clinton (former president of USA)– influence/dominance
* Barack Obama (president of USA) – influence/dominance
* Margaret Thatcher (prime minister of UK) – dominance
* Anders Fogh Rasmussen (former general secretary of NATO) – dominance/compliance
* Stoltenberg (general secretary of NATO) – Submissive/influence

Remember, these are my observations. I haven't done any formal analysis of their behavior since they haven't filled in the questionnaire. So this might reflect some sort of adjusted behavior.

Sales

Everyone goes shopping once in a while but what makes us decide what we buy? On a daily basis we buy a lot of things automatically without any deliberate thinking. We just get the milk, the potatoes, oats, and so on – the same stuff we usually buy. But if we stumble on a good offer, we start thinking about whether to buy or not. In some situations, different things happen, and that's when we have to buy things that are more expensive. This metaphor applies to sales and buying in general.

What makes the four basic styles buy like they do? It is still about their basic motivation. Let's take a look at the four styles, one by one.

The D style

- is motivated by being decisive, being the winner, looking brave, and being willing to take a risk. He is ready to make changes or more likely to initiate changes.

What will motivate the D style is

* being the first to buy a product
* being the one who buys expensive products
* being the one who buys unique products

Which relates to the snob motive and the Veblen motive from the model regarding irrational buying behavior. That means the statements that will have a positive effect on a D style could be:

* this is the newest model/version
* it is a limited edition
* this is a special model with extra features
* it is made from unique and exclusive materials
* this quality is fantastic and therefore much more expensive than our other models
* it just hit the market
* this is a rarely seen product on the market

To some D styles, the thrifty buying motive will also apply (buying cheap). But it is not the fact that the product is cheap that is the issue for a D style, it is more what can be saved that is interesting.

The I style

- will respond well to some of the same arguments as the D style but in certain situations there will be other arguments that will work better. The I style is very focused on being recognized and looking good, being popular with others. Therefore, it will appeal to the I style to acquire things that are truly unique, either because they are rare or expensive. You could argue that the snob motive more often fits the I style than the D style.

The I style could also want to identify himself with a celebrity. This means using the same products as the star or the ones the star advertises. In such cases, it's not the usual celebrity but one who is more eccentric or special that attracts the I style, so the I style is can stand out from the masses.

Statements that will have a positive effect on an I style could be:

* this product is truly unique
* the model can be fitted to your liking
* you can put together the system and accessories as you wish

The S style

- is typically motivated by something completely different: it should be safe to use the product. The product should be thoroughly tested or have been on the market for a long time and therefore used by many satisfied customers (Bandwagon motive). To the S style, it can create value if someone famous is using the product.

Statements that will have a positive effect on a S style could be:

* This has been on the market for years
* It is our most popular model
* We have a lot of satisfied customers with this product
* The production of this product has focused on safety
* The product is very reliable

WARRANTY

The S style might be the one who most often accepts arguments that contain environmental statements because the S style is strongly connected with his values and principles. This makes him different because he has this kind of interest and preference.

The C style

- is as always focused on details, rules, and being able to make an objective decision. This will most likely be seen when the product is within the C style's area of interest. This means the C style will bury himself in details, facts, tests, and analysis. If the product doesn't interest him he will make more arbitrary decisions. So, it is important to the sales person to check whether this product is within the sphere of interest for the C style.

Some C styles will be driven by the thrifty motive (buying cheap). They will typically check the market to find the lowest cost – looking for all-inclusive deals (freight and other expenses).

Statements that will have a positive effect on a C style could be:

* This model got the highest score in the test where it was up against similar products
* Here is a data sheet with the important technical information
* You can find more information and documentation in the leaflet or on the homepage

TEST RESULTS

Example
Think about buying a new car.

We cannot say anything definitively about which brand the four basic styles will choose. There will most likely be more D styles buying Audi, Mercedes, and Tesla than S styles since these brands signal power. And more S styles might buy Mazda, Toyota, and Volvo, which are brands that signal safety and security. But it is not definite that the driver of an Audi is a D style.

What we can say something about is why they are likely to have chosen this style of car and maybe something about why they chose the particular model.

The D style will probably choose a car that radiates strength and power, and says "here comes a successful winner" – or "this car owner dares to stand out from the crowd" in an old Trabant (car from East Germany before the Berlin wall was taken down) or a Hummer (big, gasoline-consuming utility vehicle when the trend is for small and environmentally responsible cars).

The powerful D style will typically choose a big model of Audi, Mercedes, or BMW. And probably the newest model. From this year. The color? Black, silver, grey, or white. If the D style is not quite as powerful and rich, he might choose the same style and model but an older one. Using the argument that others have taken the biggest loss of value (new cars reduce their value when they cross the curb outside the dealer's shop).

The I style also likes cars that radiate power and success but he likes a little more edge and extra features. The list of extra features will be pretty long, and it is not necessarily safety features that are on top. Leather seats, an extra flashy color, spoilers, and toned windows are likely so that he stands out form the crowd. The car can be like a work of art.

I styles who are not so rich will more often choose small, smart city cars like the Fiat 500, SMART, and so on. Or vintage cars that are given a shine. Speed doesn't matter as long as we are having fun.

The I style will, in some cases, choose a cheaper brand to get a bigger and more gorgeous model or more extra features.

As mentioned at an earlier stage, the S style is the style that is most likely to worry about environmental issues and will do his shopping according to this. So when the S style buys a car, he will probably choose a model that has a high mileage, emits more CO_2, and so on. If there was a car with an eco-label, the S style might choose that.

Otherwise, reliability is high on the list, as well as safety. This is why the S style often chooses brands with a reputation to turn on every time and that have lots of airbags and other safety equipment. That could be Volvo, Mazda, or Toyota.

For the C style, it is all about what is in his sphere of interest. If it is environment, he will compare these features. If it is speed and performance, that will be the focus of his investigation.

The C style will often check facts on the internet, make a spreadsheet to keep track of all the details, and make it more manageable. Maybe he will check different tests from car owner associations in other countries. All of this he will do before test-driving the cars. Again, he will be challenged by the many facts that muddy the picture and make it harder for him to decide.

But what if all four styles want to by an Audi?

The D style will typically choose one of the bigger models like the A8 or new models of Q7 or A5. Expensive cars, which radiate power and success. The car is most likely black.

The I style could choose either the smallest model – A1 because it is sort of charming and a bit naughty - or he will go for the super delicious design of A5. A different color than black is more probable here than for the D style.

The S style will choose the model that has the best match with his actual needs. It could be a station wagon with room enough for the family, dog, and luggage to be transported safely to the destination.

The C style will choose some areas that support his needs and interests. He will compare the different models according to this – quite objectively. Economy and financing will often be an important parameter.

Example

I know this guy who is an ID style. He works with communication, and he is very good at it. He gets on national TV in Denmark. He bought a new car. Big Volvo. And it was bright red with 2 white racing stripes on the hood and over the roof. I had to ask him why he chose this color? I mean, bright red is not a color that is often chosen by a male D style since it can be a little difficult so re-sell later. "Don't worry. It's not painted red – it's just a cover film. It's black underneath." So here the fun loving I style who got what he wants and the winner D style will get what he wants when the car is to be sold.

Recruiting

When tasked with choosing the right candidate for a job, how do you do so? Most often there will be qualifications and competencies that are required, but this may not be enough. When a task is motivating; we will solve this task with greater enthusiasm than if the task is not so motivating. Often, the quality of the solution will be better and the task more prone to be completed within the deadline if we are motivated. This is a good argument for within-role behavior analysis in the recruiting process.

I have been privileged to work with different national and international companies regarding their recruiting processes. This work has made me divide the interview process into three parts:

before
- everything that will take place before we meet the candidates at the job interview

during
- the interviews and everything going on in relation to the job interviews. This could include conducting tests and analysis

on-boarding
- after we decided who to offer the job to. It is a process, including coaching of managers and the like

Not all the tasks are related to the DISC model, but I will present some examples here to give you some ideas for how you could improve the process in your organization. I will only talk about these three parts, so, if you don't know much about recruiting, you might need to consult other books regarding this subject.

Before

There can be different reasons for why we think we need to recruit a new employee:

* we have discovered that we have more tasks than our present staff can handle
* one or more employees have chosen to leave the company (retirement, new job, etc.)
* we need to replace an employee who was fired (for whatever reason)

But, maybe we don't need to recruit at all.

In many companies, I have seen new tasks being handed out to the employees sort of haphazardly.

The question becomes: Who has the time to do this task right now, instead of who is motivated and has the skills and experience to solve it best. This means that it could be rewarding to take a look at the team and the distribution of tasks within the team. This is not a thing to do every month, but maybe once a year or every other year.

Depending on the sort of tasks the team is working with, this exercise might help us to be aware at all times when we place a task on an employee.

How to do this? Let the team together make a list of tasks they solve. This is a rather complicated task, so take your time. Maybe it can be an advantage to let every team member make their own list and then afterwards make the team's total list. Every task is evaluated regarding how much time it consumes, how often it is repeated, and what competencies and DISC styles would be beneficial to have when solving this.

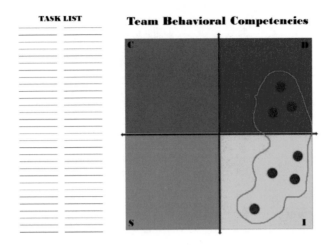

After this, you have to know the competencies of each team member combined with their DISC profiles. And then you are ready to re-distribute the tasks. Some tasks will go back to the same employee but some will go elsewhere. Maybe you will find that the team has spent time on tasks that are indifferent to the goals or that more than one team member is solving the same task (it can be quite surprising what you can learn from this exercise).

And maybe you will find that when all tasks have been distributed, you don't need to recruit after all. Or you will find a pool of tasks that will be the job for the new employee. Because no one on the existing team has the right competencies or DISC style.

When you decide that this is not the time for looking closer at the existing team you will still have to look at the tasks that this new employee has to take care of. What competencies will be crucial for solving them with the right quality and in time? These, we will name *the critical job factors*. Other competencies might be nice to have, and if the candidate has these or others, it could be beneficial for developing the job. But only if the critical job factors are met.

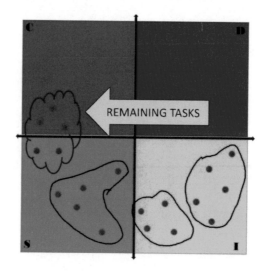

You can find inspiration for where to place the task according to the DISC model in this illustration.

When you have the complete list of the tasks in this job and have determined the critical job factors, it is time to analyze which DISC style will fit this job. Look task by task, and place them in the DISC model depending on what kind of behavior and motivation will be best to solve the task and will keep being motivating. When you have done so with every task in the job, hopefully a pattern will emerge. This pattern is the DISC style that your candidates have to match.

In the appendix to this book, you will find descriptions of 16 basic DISC styles. You can use these to find inspiration for which words will describe the DISC style you identified for a task. And it will be a very good idea to use those words in your job posting. Because the candidates that fit with this description will find them appealing and are more likely to apply than candidates with opposite profiles.

But what if there is a task that doesn't fit into the pattern? What if it is placed far from the majority of tasks? There can be different ways of looking at these tasks:

Maybe this task doesn't belong in this job?
- take a closer look at the professional competences needed to solve the

task. Do they match the other competences that are needed to solve the majority of tasks? If not, this task may not fit into this job.

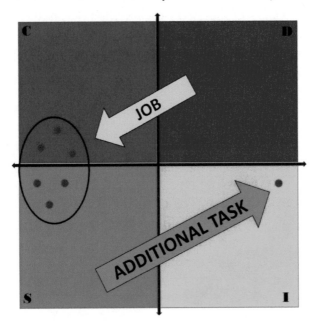

If the professional competences needed to solve the task match the other competences needed to solve the majority of tasks, it will be a good idea not to write anything about this in the job posting. It will be useful when you conduct the job interviews as a little "bomb" to surprise the candidates.

During

When you have sorted the applications, it is time to invite the candidates to the first interview. There are many ways to conduct interviews, and there are a lot of views on who should participate and how many interviews are necessary to find the right candidate.

The number of candidates to invite to the first interview depends on the complexity of the job, the level of the job within the organization, and the tradition of the organization. The first interview is about fact checking, for example, checking that the resume is accurate. In larger companies, the first interview is often conducted by the HR department.

When the candidates are invited to the second interview, it could be appropriate to include the information regarding assessments. The candidates can arrive at the interview having filled in the assessment, and the certified interviewer will then have had time to prepare the feedback session. Again, there are different views on how to conduct feedback in connection to the job interview:

*   Feedback can be done separate from the job interview and done with only the certified person and the candidate.
    This method is often used when the company's HR department takes care of the entire process until the field of candidates has been narrowed down to two or three candidates who are presented to the new employee's manager. The manager will then have a short meeting with each of the candidates and after this make his choice. The benefit of this method is that the hiring manager has to spend little time on the recruiting process.

*   Feedback can be done as a part of the job interview together with the new employee's manager.
    This method is used in all kinds of companies – also in companies with an HR department.
    The benefit in this case is that the hiring manager has firsthand information and has the opportunity to ask for more details on the spot.

On-boarding

When the choice has been made and the right candidate has been offered and has accepted the job, the time has come to think about the on-boarding process. And here the results from the analysis and assessment can be useful too.

The on-boarding process' target is to have a performing employee as quickly as possible. Some of the things that are important to achieve this are:

1st day at your new job

- Welcome ceremony with new colleagues and manager
- First introduction to tasks and goals
- Introduction to company values and policies
- Handover:
  - Computer
  - Mobile phone
  - Business cards
- Introduction to essential software systems
- Walk around the production plant with your assigned colleague
- .....

* make sure the employee knows his tasks and his objectives, and understands and accepts them

* make sure the employee knows about company policies and methods

And many companies are very good at doing this but this doesn't prevent the on-boarding process from failing sometimes, and the employee leaves the company quickly (more or less voluntarily).

There is so much more to deal with to ensure the successful on-boarding of a new employee. Because a company has its own unique culture with a lot of factors that cannot be described on paper such as an employee policy. And how is the chemistry between the members of the team, the manager, and the new employee? And how should the manager actually lead this new team member that he doesn't know very well?

I believe that the result of the assessment and analysis that were conducted previously in the recruiting process can give some valuable advice for how to solve these problems.

* Behavioral analysis can give clues for how the manager can most efficiently communicate and lead this new member of his team
* Behavioral analysis can give information regarding what kind of plan to use and how detailed this should be to make sure the first days/weeks of employment will be a success for both parties
* Intelligence tests can give information regarding how fast this person will learn, how complex of a task he will be able to handle, and, to an extent, how fast the person will solve his tasks

The different behavioral will have different wishes for the perfect on-boarding process. D styles would very much like to know the target and start working towards it straight away.

How to be

an effective leader

- for your new employee

by your HR Partner

I styles like to start quickly, too, but feel the need to get to know people first. S styles need security. They need to know who they will work with and who they can ask about all their silly questions (that everyone needs to ask when we start in a new job). And finally, C styles would like to know where to find the information needed and which quality standards must be observed.

The same thing goes for leadership. Different kinds of behavioral styles prefer to be led in different ways. To get the best from this new employee, the manager could adjust his behavior. This will ensure that communication runs more smoothly, with less misunderstandings and better performance. Here come a few pieces of advice for managers who want to adjust their behavior and communication to match the behavioral style of their employees:

Meeting D styles	Meeting I styles
* Focus on goals and results * Be fact-oriented * Be brief – don't go into too many details * Make demands and make them clear	* Be sociable – remember to small talk * Show him you like him * Remember to acknowledge him * Be brief – don't go into too many details

Meeting S styles	Meeting C styles
* Be trustworthy and a friend * Be supportive * Create a sense of security * Be available for guidance	* Focus on facts * Provide extra documentation and other written information * Provide instructions regarding deadlines and quality level

Creating the perfect team

The word *team* is used in all kinds of situations in our daily life. But when we work professionally with teams we need to be a little more specific regarding what the word actually means. A great deal of authors have given their contribution to what the word *team* means. I find that the definitions below make really good sense.

Patrick Lentioni:
"a relatively small number of people...that shares common goals as well as the rewards and responsibilities for achieving them"

T ogether

E veryone

Tuckmann & Smith:
"a small number of people with complementary skills who are committed to a common purpose, set of performance goals, and approach for which they hold themselves mutually accountable"

A chieves

M ore

But how do we get the members of the team to work well together? If they have complementary skills, they most likely have complementary behavioral styles too. And we know what will happen when a group of complementary behavioral styles has to work together...

When two opposite behavioral styles have to communicate and cooperate there is a risk that things will go wrong since they do things in very different ways. Think of a C style and a I style.

C style	I style
* Fact-oriented * Focuses on details * Prefers firm structures and rules * Sticks to rules and agreements * Prefers to work alone * Prefers written communication	* Oriented towards ideas and new possibilities * Focuses on people * Perceives rules and structure as limiting * Finds ways to go around rules * Will often prefer to work with others (or in the company of others) * Prefers to talk about things

So, to make cooperation between two opposite behavioral styles work for the better, they both need to adjust their behavior and be open to the counterpart's communication even when the other does not adjust.

But if two opposite behavioral styles succeed in cooperating, the outcome can be fantastic and very rewarding for both people and organizations. Then they will be able to use each other's strengths to obtain excellency. The individual style will have others who will cover his weaknesses with their strengths. And then 2 and 2 is no longer 4 but 5.

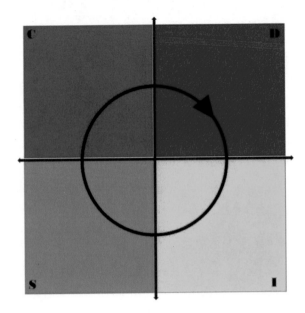

Roughly speaking we can say that in a well-functioning team, a continuous development process is running all the time. A process where D styles make decisions regarding what changes are to be made and what the goals are.

They do so based on the data and analysis that the C styles have provided through their observation of the implementation of solutions that is done by the S styles, who also take care of the more routine-oriented tasks.

Once the D styles have made the decisions, the I styles will be communicating, selling the changes and goals, and keeping up a good spirit. This is what I tried to illustrate in the figure on the previous page.

All of this is under the condition that the manager lets the team work on their own, only interfering when they ask for it or when the manager wants to recognize and praise them or support them with more information and goals.

This can be an ongoing process until extreme changes are brought to the team such as a change in team members, change in management, or leadership and so on. The author Katzenbach has written more about this subject.

Creating a team

When we have to put together a team, it is very important to be focused on the goal and the tasks of the team. Because when we work with a DISC model, we work with motivation and behavior and to use this in the creation of a team, we have to know what kind of motivation and behavior are needed. Of course, we cannot neglect the professional skills – they have to be in place, too. But don't let any of these stand alone. Let's take a look at an example:

An organization works with people in need. The board has developed a new vision, which should help the organization gather more funds and be able to help more people. But how should the vision be reached? The board wants Jock to put together a team who will work within a narrow deadline and come up with plan for the vision to give out to the entire organization.

Jock knows that Betty from HR works with Extended DISC, so he seeks her help to solve the task.

Jock:	Hi Betty. I need to find approximately 6 guys and girls who, in a short time, can figure out how we can gather more funds. The goal is € 10.000.000 in 6 months. I must emphasize that it is not this team who will do the fund raising. They will only figure out how to do it and make the action plan.
Betty:	Well, as you know, everyone who is recruited goes through an Extended DISC Personal Analysis, and we have their permission to keep this information and use it in situations like this. I think it will come in handy.
Jock:	As I see it, we need some people who can come up with a lot of good ideas and see opportunity where no one else can.

Betty:	Yes, I get your point. But the challenge is that the guys who get these great or skewed ideas aren't very good at making firm decisions that are sustainable. They might change their mind when everything has been launched or forget vital details. I think it will be a good idea to have a brainstorm with guys like this.
Jock:	And then, have others check the ideas and make them work on the details?
Betty:	Precisely
Jock:	I see.
Betty:	So let's find a C style and an S style to be coordinator and referent at the brainstorm meeting.
Jock:	And we will invite a bunch of I styles to do the brainstorm.
Betty:	I think the team should be less C styles, more S styles, and a few I and D styles. Because their task will be budgets, time schedules, marketing materials, sub-goals, training schedules for the fundraisers... Will you be a part of the team yourself?
Jock:	Not in the daily work. But I will have meetings with them to ensure motivation and that the deadlines are kept.
Betty:	As I remember, you are a DI style, right? Then you also can help them make the more difficult decisions. But you must be careful not to put too much pressure on them. That will only create fear and anxiety.
Jock:	So the plan looks like this: 1. Meeting with the entire team so they can be presented to each other, the goal, and the deadline.
Betty:	And to get to know each other. Let them do something nice together. Then you can have the brainstorm.

Jock:	After the brainstorm, they will start choosing the ideas they will work on?
Betty:	Yes. And at this point, you must emphasize that they have to choose. They cannot dismiss them all.

Leadership

In all kinds of organizations there are managers, and they all do the job in their own way depending on the current situation, skills, and training. Some say that people can be born leaders. I am not so sure. I believe that anyone can become a leader and even a good one if we want to. Depending on the company, the current situation, and the task at hand, the manager will have more or less success in leading employees. This success will often depend on the natural behavioral style of manager, his skills, his ability, and his willingness to adjust his behavior.

I have facilitated many trainings with managers and HR people, and during these trainings we have made descriptions of the perfect manager/leader, not compared to a specific situation in the organization, but just in general. What kind of personal skills and behavior styles would be beneficiary for a manager? The results have been very similar from group to group. There are no differences in geography, age, or seniority of the participants.

Here are some of the results that I have seen most often:

* Decisive
* Visionary
* Creates goals
* Follows up
* Analytic
* Empathic
* Good listener
* Follow through
* Inspires and motivates
* Ensures teams are functioning well
* Makes plans

After doing this task, I have asked the same participants to tell me how they see the strengths of the four basic behavioral styles as managers. Then, it is something like this that came up:

* Control details and time schedule * Ensure quality * Make instructions and policies * Make adjustments to plans * Plan for the long term * Evaluate * Analyze	* Create (bold) goals * Control goals * Create changes * Make things happen * Get resources for the team * Make fast decisions * Create pressure
* Make the group function * Focus on routine tasks * Care and nurture * Make sure that everyone does their part of the task * Take care of the administrative tasks	* Motivate * Inspire * Focus on optimism and positive sides * Get new ideas * Focus on the hole * Tell the good story

The pattern that emerges shows that a lot depends on the situation the organization is in. So if the organization needs major changes and focus on results, D styles are to be preferred as managers. Since it will be easier for them to make the risky decisions that are needed in such a situation, because they don't have to adjust their behavior very much to do so.

And, if the organization is in a stable environment with no major changes needed, S styles can be the perfect managers. They will nurture and care and make small adjustments along the way. S styles work very well when changes need to be implemented because they have the patience needed for the job, and it is natural for them to do what has been agreed to – if they buy in on the decisions.

We can say that:

* D styles are good at initiating changes and making decisions
* I styles are good at inspiring, motivating, and selling the decisions
* S styles are good at implementation and the routine tasks
* C styles are good at analyzing results and evaluating to ensure quality is constantly improving

This tells us that we need managers from all of the four basic behavioral style in our organizations, depending on where in the organization they are placed, which situation the organization is in, and where they want it to go.

We must, of course, remember that a manager's behavior depends on how much pressure they are under.

When we consider which behavioral style that will benefit the organization most, we could also consider how the employees prefer to be led. There are, of course, differences here, too. Here are a few statements to exemplify this:

* Wants to be left alone * Wants peace to get the job done * Wants enough time allocated to ensure a high quality in the solution * Wants a manager with high professional skills * Wants perfect documentation for any decision	* Wants be in charge – and if this is not possible, likes to get the feeling that he has big influence * Wants to create changes * Wants focus on facts and the results * Wants to be the winner – or on the winning team * Wants everyone else to work in the same way as he does

* Wants the feeling of security – changes must be announced in good time	* Doesn't want any limits
	* Wants possibility to work creatively
* Wants to be listened to/ taken into concern	* Wants a positive and optimistic environment
* Wants help when it is needed – preferably without asking	* Wants to work together with others
* Wants the manager to take account of their values	* Wants to be praised – a lot

If there is too much or too little leadership, it will affect the performance of the employee. Some behavioral styles will most likely let the manager know what is wrong, D styles especially. S styles are not likely to let the manager know either, but will suddenly leave the organization because they are fed up with the situation, even after 10 or more years of employment.

So, it will be an advantage for managers to know the preferred behavioral style of their employees – in this way, they can get a better match, and this will, in general, lead to a better performance of the organization and the single employee.

Changes

Some profiles loves change. They thrive in an environment with continuous changes. Especially D styles can find quality in the change in itself – that is, change for the sake of change. But how do the four basic styles respond to changes?

I have no doubt regarding which profile loves changes most. Big changes that is. And that is – of course – the D style. D styles are on the move, always wanting something new. They like to create new things, change the existing, which is very likely, unless they created the existing themselves... The D styles will make the decision to initiate changes and don't mind if it is a risky decision. The changes that have to be done will be told to the employees who cannot expect explanation or details on how or why. This is not important to the D styles. The focus of the result of the change is much more interesting.

Next week (or next month, or tomorrow), he might come up with new changes that interfere with the changes from last week. If this keeps on happening over and over, the old employees might start to neglect the orders for change since they know that any work will be in vain. Employees who haven't obtained this knowledge might find this behavior strange, but are likely to do the same after a short while.

Let me give you an example that a colleague once told me:

Some scientists studied monkeys. And they kept them in a cage – all together. They conducted the following experiment on the monkeys:

* In the top of the cage they would put fruit, which they knew the monkeys were crazy for.
* All of the monkeys wanted the fruit and climbed to the top of the cage. When they were trying to get the fruit – ice cold water was poured over them, which monkeys hate.
* Next time there was fruit on the top of the cage, the smart leader monkey sent the most submissive monkey off to get the fruit for the group. As this monkeys tried to get the fruit, a bucket of ice cold water is poured over all of the entire group of monkeys. Then, the smart leader monkey sent another monkey to get the fruit. Same thing happened: Everyone got an ice cold shower.

* After a while the monkeys didn't to try to get the fruit.
* Then, the scientists put a knew monkey into the cage – and took one of the old ones out.
* The new monkey saw the juicy fruit and sat off to get them. As it did so, the old monkeys started to beat him. They were sure that they would get an ice cold shower if anyone tried to get the fruits.
* The scientists repeated: 1 old monkey out and 1 new monkey in. The new monkey tries to get the fruit, and ALL of the other monkeys beat him up, including the first new monkey.
* Even if all the original monkeys are replaced with new ones, the story continues: If a monkey tries to get the fruit, the group will beat him. They don't know why, but it's obviously dangerous to get the fruit...

If confronted with this experience, the D style may react with distrust. Of course, it is this new change that should be carried out. Of course. And at once!

I styles do like changes, too. But not change for the sake of change. They just don't like to do the same thing over and over again. It feels boring and like routine. They are just bubbling with great ideas for interesting new ways of doing things. And these new ways will often result in changes.

If the I style made a decision to make a certain change yesterday, it may be forgotten today. And today, there is a new idea waiting to be brought to life. If the employees argue against this idea since it is different from yesterday's idea (and decision), the I style will argue that they must forget about yesterday because today or maybe even tomorrow will be much better. I style: "Don't you see the opportunities?"

They, themselves, see the opportunities in everything and not the details or even obstacles. The focus is on the big picture and where we can go. The question really is whether the I styles will act on the idea or will they just keep generating new ideas?

S styles do not like big changes. So, don't expect them to create them. The reason for this is the S styles' need for security. And when you have changes, you really don't know what will happen. You might know some, but there will always be things that cannot be foreseen. And these areas, which cannot be enlightened and taken care of before going into the process, are what the S styles find quite scary.

If the management forces the changes onto an organization that consists primarily of S styles, they will find an organization that is very much against the management. The S styles can get very stubborn in this situation since they find themselves under huge pressure. They will work against the changes, re-assuring each other that the old way of doing things works much better. It could be an S style who said: "If it ain't broken, then why fix it?"

But actually, S styles can be fantastic when the task is about implementing the changes that have been decided, if D styles and I styles remember to sell the change to the S styles, or even better, to involve the S styles in deciding how to carry out the changes. Let them know what result is expected and then let the S styles figure out how to do this in line with their values and principles.

If the analysis says we need to change, C styles will change, so we will reach our goals. But basic C styles don't like fancy changes. And when we consider the way C styles tend to decide, it can take a long time before they feel capable to make the decision, long after the D styles and I styles have lost their patience.

But if the D styles and C styles could work together, the C styles could feed the D styles with background information and analysis that the D styles need. It is almost a match made in heaven. Because the C styles and the D styles focus on the facts – C styles are just so much more focused on the details. The C styles are also good at planning the changes in details when the decisions have been made.

So, roughly speaking, we could say that the change agents would be the D and I styles, and the styles that are good at implementing and evaluating are the S and C styles.

Conclusion

As you can see, the DISC model is a useful way to think about planning, decision making, hiring, interviewing, problem solving, and generally making big change in an organization. Using this model will support not only HR departments and other hiring bodies, but also managers and employees. Knowing what style you are and what style others you work with are will help you adjust your behavior to get the best results. Similarly, knowing who to put on a team to get the best process and outcome, is informed by applying the DISC model.

Please remember that it is not possible to write down the full description of all the combinations in the DISC model. Every time you meet a new person or have new experiences with people you think you know, you have the opportunity to learn something new about the people and the DISC model.

If you truly want to know your own DISC style, have your personal analysis done and get feedback from a certified and experienced coach. He or she will be able to help you discover your true natural behavior and which parts of your behavior are adjustments. You can contact your local Extended DISC representative who can provide you with the necessary contact information.

I wish you good luck with your work with the DISC model – both at work and at home.

Inge Gunnersen Flindt (July, 2016)

Appendix A

In this appendix, you will find brief descriptions of the 16 basic combinations of D, I, S, and C, combined with an illustration of where in the quadrant figure you can place this particular combination.

Every description is divided into these categories:

* Motivations
* Avoidances (things they try to avoid)
* Ideal supervisor
* Communication
* Decisions
* Strengths
* Under pressure
* Development

These are not full descriptions, but are only descriptions of the 50/50 combinations. Remember that the Extended DISC system gives you 10 different profiles, for example, with the letters DI (and ID and so on). 95/5 – 90/10 – 85/15....

The Extended DISC can provide more than 1 million different descriptions – including descriptions of combinations with three of the basic styles.

D

* Motivations
  To challenge or to be challenged, winning, being in charge, no boundaries, competition to exceed former performance
* Avoidances
  Hidden agendas, undeserved praise, emotional decisions
* Ideal supervisor
  Lets him have influence on goals, gives him a feeling of being in charge and control of the process, must be able to set goals that match his ambitions and speed
* Communication
  Very direct and fact orientated, motivating others seems like a waste of time, doesn't explain, may seem short-sighted to others
* Decisions
  Sees himself as quick, bold, and good at making decisions
* Strengths
  Results-oriented, demands progress, doesn't get bogged down with people issues, initiates the necessary changes
* Under pressure
  Can create fear in the organization due to his constant and big changes
* Development
  Ask and listen more to the answers, remember that employees need to be motivated and praised, focus a little more on details

DI

* Motivations
  To be the winner and popular for it, to be accepted socially, to work independently but with other people
* Avoidances
  Working with many details in his reports, has tight rules and frameworks
* Ideal supervisor
  Needs to earn his respect, which means the supervisor should be stronger than the DI
* Communication
  Knows how to get people's attention and sell the message, making him very good at moving people to work for his cause
* Decisions
  Likes to take risks and try the unknown, makes big and risky decisions
* Strengths
  Comes up with new ideas, wants to be the winner or part of the winning team, seeks changes
* Under pressure
  Can be manipulative. Can be focused on winning the struggle for power
* Development
  Provide the competences for a task when assigning one

DS

* Motivations
  Loyalty, serious work environment, challenges, possibilities to develop own work area according to own ideas
* Avoidances
  Doesn't want to be in situations where others make a fool of him or in discussions that are too emotional
* Ideal supervisor
  Strong person with strong opinions and values who will set the goal and pace and ensure that the direction is right at all times
* Communication
  Usually very systematic in his way of communicating, focused on the goals and facts, can sometimes be quite opinionated.
* Decisions
  Can seem rather traditional and conservative in his way of making decisions, very decisive and serious
* Strengths
  He will make changes but not constantly. He is serious regarding his work and knows how to conduct a systematic development of the tasks.
* Under pressure
  Sticks to what he knows even if the surroundings change and will often fall back on his old principles. May seem quite stubborn when he is communicating
* Development
  Spend more time listening to others' considerations before making a decision

DC

* Motivations
  Prefers tasks that seems difficult and challenging so he can develop
  his competencies; really wants to work on his own to plan, develop
  and create new ideas
* Avoidances
  People who seem superficial, inaccurate, or have a tendency to be
  focused on emotional subjects rather than facts
* Ideal supervisor
  Needs to be on top of things and stick strictly to business, being able
  to communicate demands and expectations
* Communication
  Very fact oriented and has a very professional way of talking about
  matters; some people might see him as a very demanding
  communicator
* Decisions
  Can be very decisive, making fast and risky decisions, but can also
  be quite hesitant when he thinks there are more facts to be
  considered
* Strengths
  Knows what he is doing and is able to find new solutions because
  he can be very thorough when analyzing problems
* Under pressure
  Can jump between deciding and analyzing, never being quite
  satisfied with either; can seem cold and isolated to others or even
  hard and reckless, has a tendency to focus on the not so important
  things.
* Development
  Step back and look at the big picture, considering the social
  outcomes of decisions

I

* Motivations
  Being and working with others, brainstorming to get lots of new ideas, being in different tasks and environments, selling ideas or goods, getting praise even for small achievements.
* Avoidances
  Tasks that demand focus on details, being alone with a task or just being alone, a negative atmosphere or having to deliver a negative message, like firing people
* Ideal supervisor
  Needs someone who will cheer him up, give praise, and show enthusiasm at all times, presenting tasks as new opportunities rather than demands
* Communication
  Fantastic at inspiring and motivating people, getting the mood up so there can be a happy atmosphere, which useful when selling or teaching
* Decisions
  Risky or negative decisions are often postponed, as with decisions where thorough and detailed analysis are mandatory; can often change his mind because he gets new and better ideas all the time
* Strengths
  Keeps up the positive atmosphere, cheers, motivates, and inspires others. Good at staying in touch with people, has big networks.
* Under pressure
  Trusts others too much, delegates tasks but forgets to do the follow up, doesn't get the negative message delivered before it's too late
* Development
  Follow up with others and check in to see where and if progress is being made

ID

* Motivations
  Likes to be the winner, to have relations with all kinds of people, to be popular and have a high status in the environment
* Avoidances
  Detailed tasks that demand thoroughness, precision, and a systematic approach because this will frustrate and make him tired
* Ideal supervisor
  Inspires and motivates, knows which goals and visions are important, gives prestige when goals are obtained, flexible in reports so that detail is not so important
* Communication
  Pleasant to talk to as long as the subject has his interest, will be the person who gets the most attention but might not be able to listen for very long if the subject doesn't have his interest or isn't about him as a person
* Decisions
  When deciding, he will use intuition and gut feeling rather than thorough analysis and calculations, sees himself as a good, fast, and risky decision maker who takes a snap view of the situation before deciding
* Strengths
  Keeps up the positive attitude when there is progress of his liking, good at motivating, inspiring, and cheering others on to perform, good at staying in contact with all kinds of people
* Under pressure
  Can be too headstrong when it comes to changes, will jump from case to case - not completing anything, postpones things that don't have his interest
* Development
  Delegate jobs that do not keep your interest and consider facts while comparing decision options

IC

* Motivations
  Creating new stuff for others and with others, brainstorming on professional issues, positive professional environments, working with others; will be motivated when others can use his solutions
* Avoidances
  To be alone (it will seem to be some sort of punishment.), a negative atmosphere, only having emotional subjects on the agenda
* Ideal supervisor
  Gives praise and inspiration in a friendly way, will sometimes need to cheer him up regarding his professional achievements
* Communication
  Good at contributing to a positive work environment because he motivates and inspires his surroundings; is a great storyteller and can present old cases in a new way
* Decisions
  He will most often try to bring both facts and people into the decision in a way that both parties will be taken into regard
* Strengths
  Getting people into a good mood, seeing the bright side of the case and tasks, will not take stupid risks, focused on getting the wrongs corrected in a positive way
* Under pressure
  Tendency to paint a picture too perfect and be a little too kind and friendly; may talk more than he listens and not be able to work when he has been alone for a while
* Development
  Ask and listen with directed questions so as to direct conversation toward the information that fits the task specifically.

IS

* Motivations
  Needs to work with other people and will actively make contact with others, both known and unknown; positive environment and possibilities to discuss the tasks with colleagues and his supervisor to get the best solutions
* Avoidances
  Being alone for too long will be very demotivating, having to work with very detailed tasks that require a single focus over a long period of time, having to make risky decisions that will have a negative impact on people; being around aggressive people.
* Ideal supervisor
  Approachable and able to listen and help, gives praise both on the task and on personal issues
* Communication
  A positive communicator who is able to get everyone into the conversation.
* Decisions
  Will take people into consideration every time he makes a decision, but will change his mind given the right arguments, unless it is regarding an area where he has strong feelings or his principles weigh heavily
* Strengths
  Encourages others to do their best, tries to find means to improve the atmosphere and make people thrive, always in an optimistic way
* Under pressure
  Neglects signs of danger or trouble, trusts people too much, may not confront others or make even necessary conflicts
* Development
  Be sure to deal with the negative sides of a task even if they might kill the good atmosphere

S

* Motivations
  Well-defined tasks and responsibilities, prefers to have guidance from his supervisor or senior colleagues when presented with new kinds of tasks
* Avoidances
  Dishonest or disloyal people, having to make critical decisions on his own
* Ideal supervisor
  Acknowledges all the tasks solved by the S style since he often solves "invisible" tasks, provides support and guidance for making hard decisions, saying no, or engaging in conflict.
* Communication
  Prefers one-on-one communication, is very good at listening, wants to be fully prepared if he has to make a speech or lecture, can seem hesitant if the message is negative
* Decisions
  Prefers that others make the decisions if they are about critical issues; if the subjects regard an area where he has strong values or principles, he will decide more easily and stick to the decision, but if he makes decisions within his own area of expertise, he will have no problems doing so swiftly
* Strengths
  Works systematically and tries to make small adjustments to improve and not to destroy the existing structures and solutions, doesn't have a problem with solving the same kind of task over and over again
* Under pressure
  Has a very hard time saying "no" might get stuck in routines and get too easily satisfied with the standard of the work, more likely to stick to the traditions and what is known
* Development
  Ask for support when it is needed

SD

* Motivations
Knowing that he will not be abandoned or let down, having
company values and principles that are aligned with his own
* Tries to avoid
Multitasking, unserious work environments, decisions made without
taking the necessary precautions
* Ideal supervisor
Respect-worthy and ready to help and participate whenever
necessary
* Communication
When he feels he can contribute to the solution, he will present his
statement quite strongly and directly; otherwise, he will not be seen
as an enthusiastic and extroverted communicator
* Decisions
When the framework and goals are not precise or risky, he will
spend a great deal of time on deciding because there will be so much
more to take into consideration
* Strengths
He is very good at finding small errors and mistakes, works hard
and focused on his tasks, very good at planning work routines, and
doesn't leave a task unsolved or let the team be lead astray
* Under pressure
Tendency to get stuck in the routines and only make very small
adjustments, stays with people he knows and keeps a safe distance
from strangers
* Development
Step back and look closely at the bigger picture every once in a while
during smaller tasks

SC

* Motivations
Being able to concentrate on own assignments and cases, knowing exactly what is expected from him, a work environment with focus on "no mistakes," and a high degree of quality
* Avoidances
Jumping to conclusions or form an opinion quickly; carrying out others' fast and ill-considered decisions
* Ideal supervisor
Well balanced and willing to take charge when there are risky decisions to be made and who wants to take care of and help his employees
* Communication
Patient at listening, tries to analyze what his counterpart is saying, seems calm which lets others trust him, prefers to have time to consider what to say and how to say it
* Decisions
Effective and fast when making routine decisions or decisions within his own proficiency, especially if there are clear and accurate frameworks, goals, and instructions; for more critical decisions, it will take him much more time, and he may hope that others will take over
* Strengths
Will stick to the agreed upon principles even under pressure, will focus on his own task – not interfering with others and their tasks, will not make ill-considered decisions
* Under pressure
Will seem indecisive, dwelling with multiple solutions unable to choose, which will make him stuck with well-known solutions
* Development
Consider alternative and new solutions

SI

* Motivations
  A safe and known environment; planning ahead, long term
  planning, when people try hard and are persistent
* Avoidances
  Aggressiveness makes him feel anxious; others seeming restless does
  the same
* Ideal supervisor
  Needs to acknowledge and give recognition whenever possible,
  needs to be consistent
* Communication
  A pleasant communicator and debater, good at finding a balance
  between listening and talking, unplanned presentations make him
  insecure and perform accordingly
* Decisions
  Wants to take everyone into consideration when making bigger
  decisions, seems to others that he is a careful decision maker
* Strengths
  Willingness to always help others and never put too much spotlight
  on his own achievements; will do a lot and work overtime to keep
  his promises
* Under pressure
  Can seem like a slow and doubting decision maker, wants to know
  everyone's opinion on the subject and take them into consideration
  before making any kind of decision
* Development
  Make decisions on his own and be more bold

C

* Motivations
  Likes planning, making structure for the data, validating the data and checking the calculations, detailed plans make it easy to start working on the real task; if not, he will make the plans first
* Avoidances
  Aggressive people who bully others, working together with others at all times will de-motivate, as will working with emotional issues
* Ideal supervisor
  Leaves him alone most of the time, so he can focus on the task; helps with planning and setting priorities without being too specific, acknowledges him specifically regarding the task and solutions of it
* Communication
  Calm communicator who will try to stick to the facts and tasks, no small talk, surprised if others aren't as motivated as he is when he starts a detailed examination of the details
* Decisions
  Makes careful and well prepared decisions, likes to collect a great deal of information, conducts a thorough analysis and checkup before actually deciding, which he believes is the only way to get a quality decision
* Strengths
  Wants everything to be perfect or at least live up to his quality demands, has high demands, very good at finding errors and mistakes, proceeds in a natural careful manner
* Under pressure
  Gets stuck in the details, doing re-re-checks to make sure nothing is wrong; often isolates himself from colleagues who might need his work
* Development
  Remember people – they may need your support or acknowledgement without asking for it

CD

* Motivation
Well-structured and organized work environments, room for him to come with own ideas for improvements, tasks that look hard or complex
* Avoidances
Too many routine tasks and too many tasks that are just the same as usual, being pushed into taking risks, teamwork, he thinks is lazy and social people's way of doing nothing
* Ideal supervisor
Keeps track of the big picture at all times, especially when there is pressure or it is an unsecure situation
* Communication
Very fact-oriented, but you will probably have to ask for information to get it; seems short-tempered and cold to others
* Decisions
Wanders from quick and effective decisions to more objective correct decisions, making others perceive him as indecisive, changing his mind all the time
* Strengths
Gets a lot of new ideas all the time and is able to think creatively while considering the facts; seems to others that he is making improvements to familiar topics
* Under pressure
Considers leaving people alone as a good way to motivate them. This will be more clear when he is under pressure, others perceive him as inflexible and cold
* Development
Remember to encourage people and bare them in mind

CI

* Motivations
  Working with people in an open atmosphere where he can focus on opportunities and the good mood; some degree of organization is needed, so he will be able to find his place
* Avoidances
  Too many tasks that demand a great deal of focus on details and routine will decrease his motivation; the same with a very negative atmosphere or if the team doesn't accept the new suggestions and ideas he is coming up with
* Ideal supervisor
  Creates a positive and optimistic work environment to make the person feel at ease and to assure that the person is clear on his role in the team and his tasks
* Communication
  Approaches others in a positive and pleasant manner; very good at presenting facts in a positive way that will be inspiring to others; able to point out errors and mistakes in an assertive way
* Decisions
  Has a tendency to make popular decisions rather than the most objectively correct decisions, making others think that he is no good at making decisions
* Strengths
  Good at paying attention to his surroundings and taking them into consideration, likes open debates and brainstorming to some extent, good at finding errors and presenting them, so they will not go on unnoticed
* Under pressure
  Will not work efficiently and independently enough, his decisions will become vaguer, will seem even more indecisive, he may forget what the task is really about
* Development
  Remember the task. Trust the decisions he makes

CS

* Motivations
  Likes to work on his own but with the possibility to get help when needed; plans being followed strictly, a calm atmosphere
* Avoidances
  Things getting too emotional makes him stick his tale between his legs, avoids bickering and other situations that seems risky
* Ideal supervisor
  Provides a quiet working space for him, understands that this person will be contributing more in the detail area than big things
* Communication
  A very calm and modest communicator who will explain when asked, but don't expect him to stand up and sell his own ideas or give presentations when not well prepared
* Decisions
  Would rather not make decisions where the outcome is unclear, but making decisions regarding his own proficiency and regarding his own tasks is much easier for him
* Strengths
  Accepts the instructions he gets from others, especially from his supervisor, prefers being given precise quality measures to follow acts calmly and professionally
* Under pressure
  More likely to be confused by many facts and tasks, has doubts about how to proceed or to start new tasks; when exposed to criticism, he easily gets offended
* Development
  Try getting the big picture before he focusses on the details. Become more thick skinned

Appendix B

In this appendix, I have listed the characters from some TV series and movies and assessed their primary DISC style.

Bones

Dexter

Everybody Loves Raymond

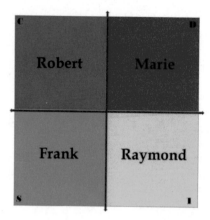

Frasier

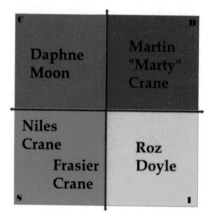

Friends

Grey's Anatomy

116

House M.D.

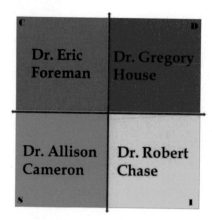

Madagascar

Olsen banden

Peanuts

Madagascar

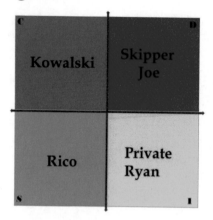

Pretty Little Liars

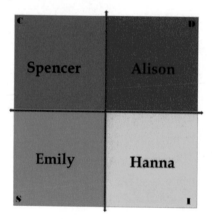

Scandal

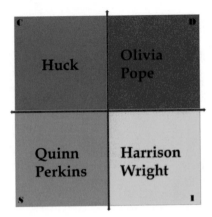

Seinfeld

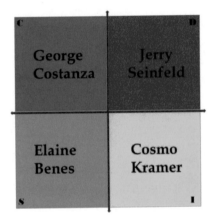

Sex and the City

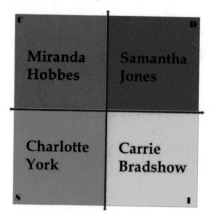

Star Trek

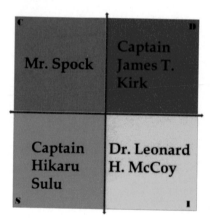

The Beatles

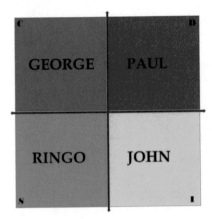

The Mentalist

The Smurfs

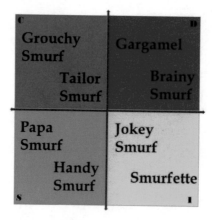

Vampire Diaries

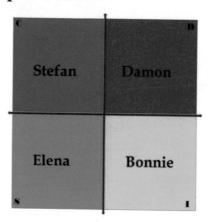

- "Show me anything. I can handle it" (*Aliens*)
- "Frankly my dear, I don't give a damn." (*Gone With the Wind*)
- "There are two men I trust. One is me and the other is not you." (*Con Air*)
- "Go ahead. Make my day." (*Dirty Harry*)

- "If I'm not back in 5 minutes, just wait longer." (*Ace Ventura*)
- "Every man dies, but not every man lives." (Braveheart)
- "Seize the day. Make your lives exraordinary."
  (*Dead Poest Society*)
- "Never underestimate the power of denial."
  (*American Beauty*)

- "I'm just your mother. You owe me your entire existence on this planet."
  (*Addams Family*)
- "I'm not a smart man, but I know what love is."
  (*Forrest Gump*)
- "Life is filled with a million goodbyes and it hurts every time."
  (*Eve's Bayou*)
- "A heart is not measured by how much it is loved, but by how much it is loved in return."
  (*Wizard of Oz*)

- "I am never late. If I am late it's because I am dead."
  (*Entrapment*)
- "The most valuable commodity I know of is knowledge."
  (*Network*)
- "Professor Marvel never guesses. He knows." (*Wizard of Oz*)
- "May the saints protect us from the gifted amateur?"
  (*Dial M for Murder*)

Index

42375500R00074

Made in the USA
San Bernardino, CA
01 December 2016